A New Crew for the Blue Emu

By Cameron Macintosh

Ruth was the boss of a fishing boat called the Blue Emu.

Ruth had a crew of strong cats.

It was true that the cats were great at pulling up the fishing net.

But when they threw the fish
on the deck,
the cat crew grew greedy!

They chewed up all Ruth's fish!

So Ruth got a new crew of dogs.

The dogs did not chew up the fish.

But when the net was in, the dog crew had a long nap!

On Tuesday, Ruth got a crew of rats.

But the rats could not pull up the net.

Ruth felt blue.

Then Ruth came up
with a good plan.

She got a few dogs, a few cats
and a few rats!

The Blue Emu's new crew did well.

Ruth's dogs and cats pulled up the net.

If the dogs were due for a nap, the cats woke them up.

Ruth's rats packed away the fish so the cats could not eat them. They had no clue!

And there were no feuds!

"Such a great crew," said Ruth.

CHECKING FOR MEANING

1. What did the cat crew do after they tipped the fish onto the deck? *(Literal)*
2. What kind of animals were on the third crew? *(Literal)*
3. Why do you think the dogs wanted to take a long nap? *(Inferential)*

EXTENDING VOCABULARY

crew	What does the word *crew* mean? What are some other words you know that have a similar meaning?
blue	Read the word *blue*. In this story Ruth felt blue. What does it mean if you feel blue? What is another meaning of the word *blue*?
feuds	What does the word *feud* mean? How might you be feeling if you are having a feud with someone?

MOVING BEYOND THE TEXT

1. Are fish always caught in nets from big boats? Where else might you go to catch a fish?

2. What are some other tools people might use to catch fish?

3. Have you ever been on or seen a boat? What was the boat like?

4. Ruth's best crew was a mix of cats, dogs and rats because they were good at different things. Why is it important to work together like that?

TIME TO WRITE

Imagine you are part of Ruth's crew. Write about your day on Ruth's fishing boat.

PRACTICE WORDS